IT'S YOUR LIFE, WHAT IS NEXT?

Bill Chapman

DEDICATION

When I began the process of writing this book, I gave so much thought and consideration as to why I wanted to do this. Well, I concluded that I wanted to present various examples of how I have been blessed and hopefully share this with others who either have or do not have a good support system in their life. Whatever your age or circumstances, you can experience a good life if sound and positive decisions are made as you go through life. As you read on, this will become clearer. My decisions were fairly easy as I had guidance and support along the way, but everyone can have great outcomes if they use good judgement, follow their right and wrong feelings, and most of all base all decisions on Godly principles. Also, if you look in the right places you can find a little friend or two who can help you down the path.

With all of that said, I would like to dedicate this writing to the six greatest influences in my life. Without a doubt the one and only greatest influence is my Lord. He created this wonderful world and everything in it which includes people. As a result of his actions the other five people came into my life and two of them were part of creating me. That would be my mother and father. God and those two people along with my wife and two children have been the people who have supported and influenced me throughout all the days of my life.

I will start with my mother and father. As you will see later, our entire family always called my mother Munnie Gal and my dad Daddy Boy. This may seem a little strange, but the story goes, that my oldest sister (Lena Ann), had heard someone say gal and boy and she had trouble with mother so she changed it to Munnie Gal and Daddy Boy must have fallen in place. From that time on everyone called them Munnie Gal and Daddy Boy. I was the youngest child of three with two much older siblings. Thus, I was a handful to manage, and both of my parents did it well and for that I am forever grateful. I cannot say enough to praise them for loving and supporting me and for that reason, I want them front and center of my dedication of this writing. Without them and my loving God I would be nothing.

Next, I would like to acknowledge my wonderful and loving wife. She is the balancing act, common sense, and level-headedness part of our marriage. She has always kept me on the straight and sensible path. For that I am so thankful. In addition to those qualities, she has always been supportive no matter what crazy ideas I have thought up and attempted to put into practice. No matter what the situation or how difficult it appeared to be, she was always at my side and for that I am grateful. In addition to those qualities, she is a great mother who loves her children, grandchildren, etc. immensely and would go to the ends of the earth for them and me. Therefore, I want to dedicate this book to my wonderful wife, Glynna, as she has played a starring role in most of my life's ups, downs, and all around and for that I am thankful.

In addition to the influences mentioned above, I have two more wonderful people who have impacted my life so much. Those are my children Kim and Will. These two characters gave me added purpose in my life and a few challenges along the way. When both of my children were born, I was shocked into the reality that I had more responsibility than ever. However, at the same time I had the greatest feeling in that now I have my own little family who I love greatly. Both of my children have grown up and have families of their own. They have both made me extremely proud and what greater good could a dad ask for.

To summarize, I dedicate this book to my Lord and Savior, my parents (Munnie Gal and Daddy Boy), my wonderful wife Glynna, and my two great kids, Kim and Will. For all of them I acknowledge that I am a truly blessed man.

CONTRIBUTORS AND INFLUENCES

When you take on an endeavor like putting your thoughts and experiences to paper one must consider how and who helped get you to this place. I have had many positive influences in my life, even too many to mention them all, but each have played a significant part in my life which has partially led me to take on this project. I will list a few, but please know there have been so many and I can't mention them all.

I would like to start with my family. I was a mischievous little boy and got into many things that could have turned out bad for me, but by the grace of God and great parents, I survived.

As I grew into adulthood, I met and married my wonderful wife. Glynna and I have been married fifty-plus years as of this writing. As any married couple we have had our ups and downs, but I have told her and many others, I would marry her a million plus times again. Glynna, has been my steady rock and has a good sense of judgement. I am the type "A" personality ready to rumble while she is calmer and makes me think more and slow down. Throughout our life together (starting at the senior prom) she has always made me feel confident and that all is going to be ok. As a result of our love and marriage, we have two great and successful children. Kim, who is a dedicated and strong-minded, successful social worker. Her profession makes me so proud that she makes a positive contribution to society. Where would people in need be without people like her? Our second child Will, has been my business partner for fifteen-plus years. He, like his mother, is my steady rock at the worksite. He has made an enormous contribution to our business and I would have had so much less success without him. As with Kim I am so proud of how he works compassionately with people. Just a little more family as I can't leave without mentioning five wonderful grandchildren who have motivated me to stay as young as possible so that I can experience the joy of being a grandfather to them. How sweet it is. Of course, I have a son-in-law, Bill, and a daughter-in-law, Kristen who make me very happy in that they love my children and are raising my grandchildren and for that I am blessed. Each of them holds a special place in my heart. My oldest sister, Lena Ann, was almost like my mother as she was sixteen years older than me, but we lost her in a fatal car accident at the age of forty-two. She was married to a retired military person and they had three children. My younger sister, Sue, also married to a retired military person is very much alive, in her early eighties, and so vibrant and active for her age. She and her husband have four children.

I have had so many positive influences in my life and I hesitate to mention them as I know that I will leave someone out. So, with that said, if I do, I ask them to forgive me. Therefore, I am going to present a few which will give you an idea of what a lucky person I am to have people like them impact my life. As you read this, I ask you to take an inventory of those that have positively impacted your life and if you can, inform them of that impact and how you appreciate and value your relationship with each of them.

I could not begin to list the contributors to my life without starting with again mentioning the most influential people of all. That is my parents. They were both strong, hardworking, God-fearing, and solid people. My mother (Munnie Gal) was quick to discipline, but just as quick to support and love you. She went to all events and athletic outings. You could count on her to be there and support you. My dad (Daddy Boy) was both my dad and best friend as I grew older. We spent a lot of time together as we both loved baseball. He coached me in youth baseball, followed and encouraged me through my high school and college career. He was a very good player himself and had a vast knowledge of the game. Even into my twenties he managed our semi-pro team, and it was a great experience. I am thankful to both and miss them daily.

My sisters were very important to me growing up, but both were years older than me and I was almost like an only child as they were grown and married early in my life. However, they were very much a part of my life and I cherished the times we were together with them and their families.

I had coaches, teachers, friends, and co-workers that I became close to and they made a difference in my life. Each, in their special way, made a difference in my direction and many times assisted me with the question "What is next?" I will only mention a few, but note that many others were present in my life. What a blessing for me.

I mentioned coaches. The one that stands out the most is a guy by the name of Joe Elrod. Now Dr. Elrod as he left coaching and moved on with his education and did great things in the area of health. Coach Elrod played and coached a ton of baseball. He played college and professional baseball. He was such an influence and mentor in my life. I could tell so many stories, but I will sum it up by saying we are to this day friends and talk often. He is a great Christian person who I am so thankful to have had in my life.

Another educator that I came to know over the years was Dr. Ted Schilling. Ted was a long-term educator and an extremely caring person for his students. Although he had some serious health issues, he was dedicated to students and those in need, up to the end of his life. He helped me greatly in understanding that what you saw on the outside wasn't necessarily what was going on within. He reminded me often that we know not from whence that student came and we surely did not know the conditions he or she was experiencing. So, he always suggested that a teacher should give the student the benefit of the doubt until proven otherwise. He was an educator with compassion.

As a teacher for many years, I learned so much as time went on. I had the great fortune of working with a school administrator by the name of Ken Payne. He was a solid leader and taught me the importance of patience and to look at the complete picture before reacting. He reminded me so much of Daddy Boy. Over the years, he has been such a good friend and leader. I worked under his supervision for many years in various capacities. I learned a great deal about leadership from him.

After retiring from the school system, I moved into another profession. This was one I never in my wildest dreams would have thought I might do. That profession was sales, and more to the point, insurance sales. That was the last thing I ever thought I would do. However, I did, and it turned out to be a very good decision. You will see more about this in future chapters. As in all my walks through life I have always been blessed with a little friend who supported me throughout. The insurance world was no exception. I met a fellow by the name of Roger Carroll who was a career insurance professional and all through the years he has given me advice and support. His knowledge of sales and people have been invaluable. To this day we talk at least twice a week although he lives in another state. I am always telling him that "we should tape our conversations as they would make a great comedy routine" and each visit with him is an adventure.

For many years, I have had a very competent, knowledgeable, responsive, and caring attorney. That may seem to be a strange description for an attorney, but he is the most well-rounded attorney I have ever met. He has been a teacher, a music minister, an insurance agent, and an assistant district attorney. His name is Larry Buquoi. I just want to note that he and I have worked together on many projects and I could not ask for a better legal mind with each of them. For all of his assistance I say thank you.

Just one more and then we will move on. I found that you always are blessed to have a person that you can go to and laugh, let your hair down, and maybe just share your good or bad days. I have just that person and his name is Will A. Rogers. Not the famous Will Rogers. His middle initials are A, so I have fun with calling him WAR. Will is a great friend whom I could call at two in the morning and he would help me no matter what. I have never heard him say a bad word, he finds good in all people, and is a strong Christian person. What a great guy to be around. He has helped me stay on the straight and narrow path as we have discussed many a topic over a good stogey.

Well, I guess that is enough about the contributors and influences in my life. I have just one more, and the most important person, my wonderful wife. This lady has put up with more stuff and craziness from me than any person should have to, but she has been with me through thick and thin and is my rock. Glynna has had many health issues and personal burdens herself, but without a doubt she is a great wife and mother. I could not ask for better. Ok I am going to stop now because if she reads this, she may think I am bragging on her and I am.

REMEMBER: IT IS YOUR LIFE WHAT IS NEXT?

FOREWARD

BY: ROGER CARROLL

I take great pleasure in writing this part of Bill's book (It's Your Life What Is Next) as I have known him for forty years plus and through many stages of both of our lives in which we attempted to navigate what was next. This question has come up many times to both of us and often we share those experiences and their outcomes. He and I have been close friends for a long, long time. With that said, I feel qualified to share the following moments with you about both Bill and this book.

Like many young baseball players, Bill had a dream of becoming a major league player. He had the desire, possibly the talent, and maybe the opportunity to fulfill this dream. But as life has it, things change, people change, and hopes and dreams change. This was the case for Bill, after playing a lifetime of baseball starting with Little League as a youngster and moving on to High School, College, Semi-Pro, and a few offers from professional league teams he realized the cost outweighed the benefits at the time so what came next took a different direction in his life.

Like most of us his initial dream was followed by many "what is next adventures". Bill went on to teaching, coaching, and administration within a few school districts and retired from that career after twenty-five years. During his tenure, he made many friends, hopefully positively influenced numerous students, and contributed to society.

His next adventure and challenging time came from an area he least expected and that was another twenty-five-year career in the insurance industry. For this I take some credit as my longstanding career was in this industry and I think he finally realized what I had been telling him for a long time and that was he should take a hard look at the field of insurance as I thought he would do well in it. As usual, I was right again ha. ha. This career included a long-time partnership with his son in forming and managing a successful agency that offered employee benefits to their clients.

Throughout most of Bill's teaching career, and even into his insurance career, he established and conducted a program for DWI offenders, Defensive Driving offerings, insurance pre-licensing training, and anger management classes. All of these shared the same theme of "helping people enjoy a better life". He often shared with me the challenges that many of his participants faced, and he hoped that these programs made a difference.

Bill's entire life has been a work in progress. He has never been satisfied with the status quo. As long as I have known him he has always sought ways to use his God given talents to help people. He continues to be a coach in all aspects of his life by helping people become the very best they can be.

My friend Bill continues to dream and ask the question of what is next. I know at present he is looking for the next challenge, knowing that he still has things to accomplish. I have noticed over the years that everything he does relates to helping people and the world become better. I know that it is not about him, but rather about others that he is concerned with.

This book “IT IS YOUR LIFE WHAT IS NEXT”, is his attempt to get people to think about and plan what happens in their life. He wants people to organize and direct their lives rather than just going through life with no direction. Also, because Bill is so concerned about others and how I have seen him putting his life plan into action, I am truly honored to call him my friend and write this foreword address. I know something good is going to come from this publication.

Bill’s Longtime Friend

Roger Carroll

CONTENTS

INTRODUCTION

The past is gone, the present is a work in progress, and the future is unknown and yet to be determined. So, we really have only the present and the future under any of our control with the present being action at the time and the future being controlled by our hopes, dreams, plans, and God-given talents and direction.

WOW, what a summary of life in a few words and sentences. However, those words do really sum up life and give us only two options for what is next, either in the short run (our next second) or the long run (our future and longevity). This is the overall concept of this writing which I have given the title of "IT IS YOUR LIFE WHAT IS NEXT". This is a very important question that all of us must ask ourselves at some point and time. Some of us will take it very seriously and spend time and energy dealing with our daily activities and being concerned about the future. Others may take a lesser approach, living day to day letting life happen and hoping for the best outcome. I feel that the latter position is less productive and could be dangerous with the results being an unhappy and unfulfilled life.

Therefore, the ultimate purpose of my writing is to encourage people to become aware of where they have been in life, where they are presently, and what is next for them. It is only natural to take the easy way and have some days of concern and other days of less concern. Hopefully, after reading about these topics to be presented, per the table of contents, each of us will give a little more attention to the now and the future. If that is the end result, then our lives will hopefully become more organized and we will find reason and direction to our future. In other words, maybe more thought will be given to what is next, what is my purpose, and how do I interact with people and just maybe I can ensure that I am making a difference rather than just existing. If more of us took this approach life could be better for all.

With all of this said, I hope you enjoy the reading and really look at what is next as this question is important to each of us. When we do this we may find that life can be good (not all of the time but the majority of the time), we can be happy (not all of the time but the majority of the time), we can be productive (not all of the time but the majority of the time), and our lives can make a difference (I think this one could be most of the time).

Thanks for reading, I hope you enjoy it, and don't forget

"IT'S YOUR LIFE WHAT IS NEXT"

Chapter One

WHY DID I WRITE IT AND WHY SHOULD YOU READ IT?

I have looked back over the years of my life and have observed the changes in our society. Some of these changes are good and wonderful while others are bad and dangerous. These changes are affecting people's lives of all ages, ethnic backgrounds, religions, and they do not discriminate with respect to the part of the world in which we call home. There are many things evolving moment by moment that can, and probably will, affect both long- and short-term quality of life, not to mention our behavior with other human beings. Just to name a few, respect for each other, honor of the elderly, it is all about me attitudes, the impact of technology, how gadgets, deceptions, and the obscene are often replacing worship and dependence on THE LORD.

As we grow older, we tend to think that the good old days were perfect and wonderful. Some of that is true, but many things today make life much easier, safer, and more productive. It reminds me of a friend I was talking to, who is a little older than I am, and we were discussing the good old days at which time he brought me into focus with his opinion. He said that he loved it back in the day, but he could not understand why everyone was getting so excited about old stuff and antiques. He said, I grew up with that stuff and it is old like me, what I really want is new, shiny, clean, and pretty, you know the new stuff that is almost maintenance free. I thought to myself, he has some very good points. I think what we miss the most is the good times with family and friends who are no longer with us, and not necessarily the old stuff.

Let me get back on topic now with why I wanted to put these thoughts and ideas into print. Over the last few months, I have been sitting in church thinking and listening. Yes, me, the big sinner is doing this. For quite some time I have felt an inward tug to put these thoughts on the table and maybe even share them verbally when I have the opportunity.

I want to also note that this is not saint Bill sharing thoughts so that I can fix the world. Rather, this is old Bill trying to share a few little words of wisdom based on my experience through seventy years of life plus. It is my opinion that too many older people tend to criticize the youth of today and not get involved in making a difference. Armchair quarterbacking is the easiest position on the team, but what really makes the team great is using your talents to move the team forward.

We must remember the youth of today are a direct result of the people who influence them. This is probably one of the most difficult times in the history of mankind to be either a parent or a child. For that matter, it can even be really challenging if you live alone and have only yourself to take care of.

Young people are also growing up in difficult times in that they are more aware than us older people of the good, the bad, and the ugly parts of life. Back in the day, probably the worst thing that happened on the school campus was a student was chewing gum and maybe a few boys in high school were smoking in the bathroom. Today many students are dealing with alcohol, drugs, premarital sex decisions and much more. Kids must be stronger than ever to turn out to be sound and productive citizens when they arrive at adulthood. Adults must be the leaders in helping kids become productive, strong, Godly, and good adults themselves. I think, in general, adults are failing, not children.

At one time, I worked with the highest risk children in a particular school system. They were the worst of the worst with respect to behavior and academic performance. We were the last stop before they were being booted out of the school system completely. If they are booted who wins? No one, not the student, not the parent, and certainly not society.

They were good kids who came from bad situations and the big problem was that the grownups in their lives either struggled with finances and/or relationships, could not provide, or just did not care about giving these children guidance and love. Love and caring are key to the success of any relationship and in particularly raising children.

When I say that these were good kids, I will go even further in saying that I think that most of our society members are good people and want to do good things. They just need help and direction. It is so easy to get off track and become selfish with an all about me attitude. I remember asking every student in our intake interviews, "do you want to fail", and I can tell you not one of them said yes.

Maybe us older folks need to get out of the boat and start swimming in the water and bring them a safety net of care, love, and concern. This explains why I want to put all of this in print and share my thoughts and experiences. Another explanation is that I hope and pray when I lay my head down for the last time, that maybe, just maybe, I did not go through life only sucking up air and enjoying the beauty of this wonderful world. Hopefully a difference was made for someone because of some little thing that I did. We should all remember that a bunch of little things can turn into a huge, big thing.

Therefore, maybe it would be a good idea to look back at the title and decide. It is your life, now what? We are never too young or too old to ask this question. Maybe it is time that we evaluate where we are in life and decide what is next for us with respect to personal relationships, career choices, your gifts/talents, and your spiritual position? All of this is totally in your hands, and we must remember that choices result in consequences. These consequences can be good, bad, and may not only have an impact on you, but also on others. SOMETHING TO THINK ABOUT.

So, the bottom line about why I put all of this in print is that I hope it will motivate the reader to look at their life and evaluate their present position then take the challenging step of planning what is next. I truly mean strategically planning with respect to experiences, abilities, hopefully the desire to help people and the goal of making a difference. WE NEED TO REMEMBER IT IS NOT ALWAYS ABOUT US.

That explains why I wrote it and now let's talk about why you should consider reading it. That is quite the topic within itself. So, I will attempt to address that point by providing a little insight into human nature and the traits of us human beings in general.

Human nature is a force to deal with. It can make us selfish, unconcerned, lazy, and many other things related to non-production. We tend to take the shortcut and just hope that all works out.

I truly believe that most people are good people with good intentions. We just get caught up in daily living with the goal of survival. That is where the book comes in. It will challenge you to stretch and be more than you think you can be by pointing out the fact that we need to see where we are and plan for where we are going. Hopefully, it will make you think, plan, and act no matter what your age, financial position, or talents are.

So, dig a little deeper into this thing and see what you think. You may be surprised at how you may navigate your future. After all you are in charge.

REMEMBER: IT IS YOUR LIFE WHAT IS NEXT?

Chapter Two

LIFE - WHAT IS IT

We hear the word life used quite often and in many situations. Things like "life is good", "I had the life scared out of me", "enjoy life", and the like. I guess the real question is "What is life"? Well, Mr. Webster, in the dictionary, has a variety of definitions, and the Bible also has quite the insight into this topic. What do you say life is?

Once life has been defined, then a question is asked that is causing quite a stir throughout our country. When does life begin? If you think about it, all of those saying abortion is ok are themselves living and breathing people because of birth. Isn't that interesting? I am not going to jump off into this issue as much time, opinion, research, and philosophy could be used up if I did. Therefore, for the purpose of this publication, I will say your beliefs and thoughts about this issue are the "now what" part of the title of this writing. Remember, IT IS YOUR LIFE, NOW WHAT?

If you are a young person you are going to have many opinions to form, beliefs to acquire, and decisions to make as you go through this thing called "life". All those decisions are going to be based on your opinions, beliefs, and experiences. Therefore, in my opinion we need to get them in line with good, safe, happy, and Godly living. The decisions you make will result in your actions and thus the consequences of your actions will then be evidenced.

Good decisions relate to good outcomes while bad decisions result in bad outcomes. I think that one of the most difficult things that our God placed on human beings is choice. To magnify this difficulty, we live in a free country that encourages and supports massive freedom. This freedom revolves around actions and speech. Something to think about is how many people are harmed, both physically and emotionally, due to others having this freedom to act and say things that affect all of us? It is our responsibility to treat everyone in the manner that we would like to be treated. Young people, the most important thing I can share with you is that you must get the facts and act responsibly when interacting with other people. Think before you speak or act. Feelings, outcomes, and relationships depend on it.

If you are an old person (not sure what that number is) you have experienced opinions, beliefs, and decisions and hopefully more are to come. I guess that the older crowd needs to do a little soul-searching, status evaluation, and see if you are in line when it comes to life's desired outcomes. What is life about for you and where do you want to go from this point forward? We can't change the past, but we can surely make the future better and brighter. When looking into the future, I can't say enough about the experiential knowledge an older person has. These life experiences can and should be shared with the younger ones. Grandchildren, young friends of the family, and those you may come into some type of contact with should be in your bull's eye. Don't be afraid to make a young friend and share life with them. I know that it is a challenge in today's times but be brave and make a difference. You know, depending on age, an older person could interact with a young adult. What a tremendous opportunity to share with someone as they are going through the ups and downs of life just like you did.

I think that one of the greatest things an older adult can do for a younger person is to help them through what that young person may see as an unmanageable crisis in life. As an old teacher, I have seen young students (middle-school through college) face one of the first hurdles of life and fall apart. They have never experienced the valleys and the mountaintops of life. Therefore, the first valley throws them into a tailspin, and they feel life is over and done. This is usually the case in relationships that go south. Sometimes they just can't see the forest for the trees. Wouldn't that be a great time to share your experience and assure them that the sun will return tomorrow, the moon will shine this evening, and just maybe this would be an opportunity for that young person to begin or strengthen their Godly relationship?

This thing or experience we call life is a wonderful thing. When we really sit back and look at it, truly life itself is amazing. If we work at it, plan for it, allow it to unfold, and study its Maker, that journey can be and will be the most beautiful road that we could only imagine on this earth. Each day has both it's good and difficult moments, but think about it "Life is how we manage it" and if done well then WOW…

REMEMBER: IT IS YOUR LIFE WHAT'S NEXT?

Chapter Three

FEAR

This chapter is going to be relatively short, but the topic is a very important part of making decisions. This topic relates to something that we all experience and will continue to experience throughout our lifetime. It is an emotion called fear. It comes in many degrees and is caused by a variety of situations and conditions. The following is a short list of a few examples that could cause fear which will always impact outcomes.

1. A sudden, startling event or surprise
2. Something that causes you to think about a fearful place or object.
3. The unknown
4. Something that happened in your past.
5. A decision you must make for the future.

Many other situations could cause us to think about or experience the emotion of fear. Fear can be good or bad. The body reacts to this emotion in many ways which includes an adrenaline rush which may result in a sudden surge in strength and speed. This may be advantageous or detrimental to the situation. In the area of fear being a bad or negative thing, it may cloud the decision-making ability resulting in a bad or even a life-threatening outcome. Therefore, we can see from our brief look at fear that it is a very important factor that could seriously affect the decision-making process.

About the overall topic of our life and what is next, fear can play a major role in how we handle this emotion and how it affects decisions. It is probably safe to say that decisions relating to career choices, what you like or dislike, religion, your choice of friends, will not be impacted by a sudden startling event or a fearful place/object. This statement may not be one hundred percent true but probably a good guess.

When making future decisions concerning what is next in your life, fear of the unknown or something from your past could become a major contributing factor which probably has to be confronted and dealt with in some form or fashion. How that is done is your choice as you know your situation best.

The unknown is the most difficult of all to deal with. Many times, at best it is a guesstimate. Earlier I shared the fact that I am a Christian and lean on those beliefs which have guided me through many dark, difficult, and challenging times. Where you go for help in this area is your choice, but for me there is by no means nothing better than Christianity. Another thing related to the unknown is to do your research. The more you know the easier the decision and definitely the better the outcome. There is an old saying that relates to knowledge and I am not sure where it comes from but it mentions that the more knowledge you have the more power you have over the situation. This sounds good to me and makes perfect sense.

As we deal with fear, we must remember a few things that are very important to the topic. First, be careful and not let fear take total control of you or your thoughts. Fear can consume you which could result in terrible outcomes. Therefore, we must deal with it by either seeking professional help or possibly working through the fearful matter in a meaningful way that fits the situation. Just a friendly bit of advice, if fear is a problem in your life or someone's life that you know, share those thoughts and feelings with someone and don't let it fester into a larger problem.

Second, as we make decisions about what is next in our life we must not let fear hold us back. Fear can cause a shutdown which could result in us not reaching our potential. It can be a major roadblock that could cause us not to reach our full potential and maybe even worse, causing us not to experience our God given gifts that means we may not make a difference in our community or who knows maybe the world. I truly believe that we were not put in this world to only eat, sleep, breathe, or take up space. Each of us, and I mean everyone, has both a talent and a reason for living. With that said, we should not let fear scar our lives or get in the way of us being us and doing good things while on the planet.

REMEMBER: IT IS YOUR LIFE WHAT IS NEXT?

Chapter Four

LIFE IS GOOD

Life is good most of the time and we should enjoy those good times and not forget them. If we are not careful, we can get caught up in our human nature related to negativity. You know the old saying the glass is either half full or half empty and we can choose the status of that glass. We very seldom do this, but I challenge you to go back over the last year and list all the good things that happened to you and dwell on them for a little time as we may be surprised at the number of good things that we experienced and how reflecting on them can be so refreshing.

Life itself is good, but we must be extremely careful about falling into the negative thinking trap. Research tells us that negativity affects our body chemistry and that laughter is not only good for the soul, but also the body physically, emotionally, and mentally.

Now, how can we make life good? This may be the magic that we must work on. I think that just maybe making life good has to do with things like having a positive attitude, making good decisions, adjusting properly to failure, realizing we are not perfect nor are the other millions of people in the world, and knowing that all days will not be beautiful, but work to make those days the best that they can be for you and those around you. These are just a few of the things that make life good and I am certain that you can add much to this list. However, I have chosen these few as examples and I would like to elaborate on each in the following paragraphs.

Let's discuss our first good life topic "Having a positive attitude". Throughout my lifetime I have been around many people of which some were mostly negative thinkers, some were mostly positive thinkers, and some moved back and forth given the circumstances. Many of us fall in the later position, but all of us tend to have an overall dominance of one or the other.

I have to say that being around a person with a positive attitude certainly is more enjoyable than being around one with a negative attitude. As I think back on experiencing time with a friend of mine who always looked at situations with the attitude that the glass was half full, I remember what a joy it was to see him always thinking of the positive. My little friend always said that no matter what the circumstances, if money could fix the problem, even if you did not have the money at the time, this was not a real problem. I have never forgotten that and over the years I have tried to apply that mindset and when I did, life was always much better. Without a doubt positive thinking makes life better.

The next topic relating to what makes life good is one of "Making good decisions". I have used this topic of discussion many times in my teaching days by reminding students that good decisions equal good consequences and bad decisions equal bad consequences. This is a simple fact. Outcomes are directly related to the decisions we make. We also should note that decision-making should be based on good information that is factually based. If we do not have good info to decide, then we should do our best to wait until we do have that info. This is sometimes difficult with respect to timing. However, we should be very careful about making rash and quick decisions based on emotions only.

It is very important that we give good decision-making skills much thought and consideration. In fact, we should make this process a high priority and work diligently on developing this skill. I do not know for sure whether this is innate or learned, but I do know that we can get better at decision-making if we think about the situation at hand and use good judgement to the best of our ability. Deep into our soul we know right from wrong and we should listen and respond properly to that little voice. When we do this our outcomes and consequences will probably be good ones.

"Adjusting properly to failure" is another matter that we will address related to a good life scenario. Our first thought relating to failure is usually not positive, but failure is part of life and we must all learn to deal with it and that is usually difficult.

I am willing to bet that most successful people have experienced some form or fashion of failure. Life is like an athletic event in that you will not always win, but sometimes you do. I had a little friend who told me that it is not about getting knocked down, as that will happen, rather it is about getting back up and what happens after that. In my opinion that is great advice and a great point about adjusting properly to failure. It is going to happen, but what are you going to do about it? THAT IS THE QUESTION.

Another consideration is "realizing that we are not perfect nor are the millions of people around us". WOW, this topic can be challenging. As a teacher, I have found that most teachers tend to talk more and listen less. This is just the nature of the beast because their job is to give information and take a leadership role in molding their student's outcomes related to the subject at hand.

Type A people are taking charge of people and just maybe tend to be perfectionists and with that comes the possibility of having difficulty in dealing with others that are not of the same makeup. After being tested and reviewing my personal situation, I have concluded that I fall into that category and for that I certainly apologize to all that I have offended or affected over the years. Please be assured that most of the time I had good intentions. I would love to plead ignorance concerning this matter, but I cannot.

It is not just type A people that have difficulty in dealing with perfection issues. Many people have issues with this given their environment, upbringing, and maybe they are dealing with issues like an inferiority complex or other life-altering situations. This is something that we need to keep in mind when we are interacting with others. We just do not know what is going on with that person from an experiential, emotional, or mental position. Be careful in judging a book by its cover. This reminds me of when I was working with at-risk students. One day a prospective student walked into my office and I began the enrollment and assessment process. In looking at her record she was doing extremely poorly in school, her grades were terrible, her behavior was bad, and she was sent to us because she was being recommended for expulsion and we were her last option. After digging further into her case, I found that she was living with her elderly grandmother, her dad was in prison, and her mother had been murdered. My heart sank for this child and I certainly understood her behavior due to her situation. I hope and pray that she got better, but I don't know as we only worked with her for a short time.

To sum up this topic, I would say that we should be careful about quick judgements and work hard at giving a person a chance past the first impression. I can tell you from personal experience that most of the time my first impression was usually wrong, but I am working hard at trying to overcome this flaw which is one of the many facets of my character that makes me fall into the category of not being anywhere close to any part of perfection. This may apply to you also.

Well, this brings us to the final topic on my list which relates to "knowing that all days will not be perfect", but we should work at making them, even the bad ones, the best they can be. This reminds me of a little friend of mine who said that when we are having a bad day, we have the right to be down, feel sorry for ourselves, complain, gripe, and just know that the day was bad. However, after about twenty-four hours (a legal day) we must get up, dust ourselves off, and get back in the game otherwise this bad day could possibly turn into a bad lifetime.

We should remember that all of us will experience bad days, good days, and everything in between. Something that really concerns me is how young people view the bad days and the difficult things that happen to them. The young are inexperienced and raw when it comes to life. They have not experienced the ups, downs, and all arounds of life as those of us who are older have. This also reminds me of another little friend that gave me some good advice. He would say, when I was dealing with a hardship, "Bill do not forget that the sun will come up tomorrow and we will have a new day and a new opportunity". That was great advice and I have never forgotten his words.

Back to our youth dealing with a bad day and difficulties. My worry is that their lack of life's experiences allows them to think that the first obstacle is the end of the world which it is not as it is only the beginning. This is when I feel strongly that us older adults need to step up and offer love and guidance to them. Hopefully, those young people will have someone who cares enough to do that. This is my concern about all the at-risk kids. Maybe as adults we should quit focusing on our future or present retirement and share some of our knowledge and experiences with younger folks. WOW, what a crazy thought.

We should remember that life is good and we have control of how we view life each day. Guess what? The way we view, portray, and live life is not just about us, but rather we impact all of those around us whether we realize it or not. We do not live in a bubble. We influence those we love, work with, go to church with, socialize with, and everyone we meet. This is an awesome responsibility and one we should take seriously. MAYBE WE SHOULD TAKE THE HIGH ROAD, SHARE IT, AND ENJOY THE GOOD LIFE.

REMEMBER: IT IS YOUR LIFE WHAT IS NEXT?

Chapter Five

LIFE IS BAD

Well, we have discussed the idea that life is good and yes it is. However, maybe we should investigate the fact that sometimes life can be difficult, challenging, awkward, and maybe just downright bad from our perspective at that time. Sometimes we find ourselves in a situation that is heartbreaking, lonely, or sad. This is when life really gets us down. We have all experienced these feelings from one degree to another.

Some of those feelings come from relationships or lack of relationships. Many are the result of some type of experience either with other people or in certain circumstances. When we have these feelings maybe the answer is to remember it is your life and ask what am I going to do next given the situation. We know the answer to this is not easy and I would like to take the liberty at this time and ask that when in these challenging circumstances refer to the chapter about God. A little friend once told me that life is much better with Him than without Him and I can testify to that truth.

This publication is not all about me, but when I have the opportunity, I like to share some of my life's experiences with my readers. After all, I have probably lived longer than most of you so why shouldn't you take advantage of these ups, downs, and all arounds that I have been through?

Now, I would like to share that I have had many bad experiences in my life some of which I could not understand at the time and others were truly mistakes on my part. Some of those not only impacted me, but also my loved ones and friends. I will not go into the details of each, but I will give you a short list of some of my bad life experiences which came in various forms with varying degrees of impact. The list below is not in any order related to the personal impact on my life as each had their respective personal hardships and pain. Some of my difficulties and bad life experiences are as follows.

1. I lost my oldest sister at the age of 42 in a fatal car crash.
2. We lost my brother-in-law at the age of 29 to suicide.
3. My mother-in-law died at the age of 58 from alcoholism.
4. My father-in-law died at the age of 55 from leukemia.
5. I had a brother-in-law severely wounded in Vietnam.
6. I lost both of my parents in their 70's due to illness,
7. My wife developed breast cancer in her early 40's.
8. I lost vision in my right eye due to an accident.

9. I struggled for some time in making a career decision.
10. I had difficulty with my relationship with God because of the above things that happened to me.

Given the list above (which is not an exhaustive one) it seems that I had my share of challenges and experience with life being bad. I do not intend this to appear to be a pity party, but rather an explanation that all of us are going to experience the bad side of life, but if we handle it properly, we can work through and deal with it. We must remember that through His grace, guidance, and love coupled with our participation this too will pass and all will be better. When I say better, I do not mean to imply that the pain and suffering vanishes, and we are as good as new. What I do want to imply is that we can tolerate the circumstances and yes move on to the question related to what is next in my life.

As I review the challenges listed above, they each are a reminder of how life can be painful. With that said, we can ask ourselves how we handle these types of circumstances. Do we fall apart, run for cover, hate the world and all that is in it, or do we take that negative and painful experience and turn it into something that makes us a stronger and better person? That is a little easier for me to say after years have passed from each of these events and time has healed some, but not all the pain has vanished.

Well, I would like to take one of these ten and give you an example of how I truly believe that God works in mysterious ways. Sometimes we have a difficult time believing that, as we are all naturally selfish, and do everything only about us and us alone. The one bad day that I would like to present more details about is that of losing my sister in a car crash at the age of 42. She was married to a retired military person, and they had lived all over the world. Upon his retirement, they decided to move back home and be close to the family. That made everyone happy, and the future looked bright.

However, one Sunday afternoon they attended their oldest child's birthday party. On the return trip home, they crossed over a flat railroad track and one of the rear tires on their car blew out throwing them sideways into oncoming traffic. The initial impact centered the door on the passenger side where my sister was seated, and she was killed instantly. My brother-in-law who was driving their car sustained injuries and my niece and nephew (her children) were in the back seat and were severely injured with broken bones, cuts, and bruises. They were not able to leave the hospital and attend their mother's funeral. How sad and on that day, and many days to come, life was difficult for all of us.

My sister and I were sixteen years apart and she was almost like my mother rather than my sister. When I received that terrible phone call it was the last news I expected to hear from the caller on the other end of the phone. Once I gained my composure and began to think about all concerned, I had to do the worst thing I have ever done in my life. I had to go and give this terrible news to my parents. I asked God to give me the courage, strength, and words to accomplish this horrible task and as always, He did.

There is much more that I could share about this circumstance making life bad for me, but rather than that, I want to tell you about the long-range results of how God used me and this tragedy for the good. By no means am I downplaying the impact of this tragic event on all concerned, but it is a good example of what happens when we ask about it being my life and what is next.

After a few years passed, I decided to move to a larger city where my youngest sister Sue lived, and I encouraged my parents to do the same. They agreed and once again we were living together in the same close vicinity. This felt right to me, and it eventually proved to be a good decision. Again, I could write another book on the details related to this decision and how the lives of me and my family were positively affected, but for succinctness, I will not add that additional chapter.

Now, let's get to the culmination of much time that passed following our tragic loss and how I have had the opportunity to share that experience in hopes of preventing others from having such a bad day happen to them.

I would first like to say that the crash that took my sister was not alcohol or negligent related, it was a true accident as a result of mechanical failure. The reason I say this is that the next in my life came years later in the form of working with many, many, many DWI and other traffic offenders.

How this all came about was that I began teaching in the local school system and became involved on a part-time basis with the system's continuing education programs which included their traffic education courses. It was the beginning of me having the opportunity to share my painful story with many. Most people believe that none of these things will happen to them as they are special. Well, I was quick to inform them as to how untrue that feeling can be.

During the time that I was working with the continuing education program in the school system, the state legislature passed the first DWI law in the state which required an offender to participate in a court-approved alcohol education program. Most court systems in the state had no idea of how to implement such so me and my little friend got busy trying to help as many as we could establish a functional and productive program. From that point forward our program hopefully educated people about the need to take driving seriously from both the drinking and driving aspect as well as just being a safer driver and knowing how those driving decisions could have an impact on so many people.

Again, I will not go into the many aspects of how we educated people and hopefully changed some behaviors related to safe driving, but I will say not one audience I ever addressed failed to hear the pain, sadness, and suffering experienced by the loss of my sister that bad day. Hopefully, it was taken to heart and lives were saved. I will never know that answer, but that is what happened next in my life regarding that bad day.

The question now relates to what you and I are going to do with both past and future bad day experiences. It is important not to forget that we have choices and good choices result in positive consequences.

REMEMBER: IT'S YOUR LIFE, WHAT IS NEXT?

Chapter Six

LIFE DECISIONS AND CONSEQUENCES

This is one of the most important topics in this writing, in my opinion. This topic gets down to the real meaning of the question related to it is my life and what is next. The past cannot be changed, the present is a work in progress, but the future needs some serious thought. This is not a topic that should be taken lightly but rather one that should be given a great deal of consideration.

Often people have a natural tendency to not think or worry about what is next and take the approach of sticking their head in the sand and hoping for the best. In other words, oh well let's see what is going to happen. Sometimes this may work given the short run, but looking at the big picture, this can be both dangerous and very unproductive. Planning and following through with those plans are very important when considering the future. The consequences of planning, or the lack of it, can either be productive or non-productive.

Let's take a look at good planning that hopefully results in positive consequences. I am not sure if planning is a learned or innate skill. I do know that some people are more prone to planning than others. However, I also know of people who have picked up the skill and have made it a habit and experienced positive outcomes.

Good planning forces one to think and develop something I call forethought. Forethought forces us to think ahead and even ask ourselves the what if questions which results in deeper consideration of outcomes and consequences. If we plan well and make every effort to research possible consequences, we may avoid surprises. As mentioned in another chapter, we may then avoid the experience of fear brought on by a surprise. Fear affects decision-making. Well thought out plans that are properly executed usually result in favorable consequences and remove that fear.

Poor planning or no planning on the other hand, may result in bad, negative or unfavorable consequences. Often, we fail to plan because we want to forget the time and energy needed to plan. Other times we may feel that planning is not needed, and we will take our chances with the outcome. Whatever the reasons, many times human nature takes over and we become unconcerned or lazy and just do not take the time or make the effort to plan.

God gave us the ability to make decisions. All decisions lead to consequences be they good or bad. By no means do I have the statistics of how many decisions, on average, a person makes in their lifetime, but I feel comfortable in saying that we can all agree on a very large number. Again, I do not have the percentage of those decisions that have a positive or negative outcome. However, I will say they all had some form or fashion of consequence.

I think that we will all agree that we are hoping for good outcomes so that we can live a comfortable, safe, and happy life. To accomplish this goal, we need to make good and sound decisions as often as possible. The scary thing is that the decisions we make and the consequences that result from those decisions don't only have implications for us but many others around us. This is something to think about given the fact that our basic nature is to be selfish and have all things be about us.

Who are the others that fall under our umbrella of influence? The obvious are our family and friends. What about those we work with, casual acquaintances, and those we don't know about but see us in action?

The consequences I am talking about are things that impact and affect all of us like family matters, school issues, work issues, professional decisions, health decisions, our attitude about certain things, language, habits, how we treat others, dealing with difficulties, handling success, life in general, the reality of death, and many more that appear throughout our lifetime. These are all related to decision-making and things we will deal with at certain times within our life.

That said, we need to go back to our general theme. It Is Your Life What Is Next? Whatever stage of life you are in you must, and will, make this decision. We can all be assured that consequences will follow all decisions. You and I may address these life issues based on sound planning, poor planning, research, a gut feeling, a Godly relationship, or any other means at our disposal. I don't have that answer, but each of us needs to find it so that we can make good decisions with good consequences. This result would have such a positive impact on all.

REMEMBER: IT IS YOUR LIFE WHAT IS NEXT?

Chapter Seven

WHAT ABOUT PEOPLE SKILLS AND THEIR VALUE

We all are given gifts and talents. Some maybe more than others. There are many talents that I do not have, and one is musical. I can't play a musical instrument, my singing is less than good, and I know nothing about reading music. So, with all of that exposed, I think it is safe to say that music is out for me except for one aspect and that is I enjoy music. I like all types of music including the oldies, country, gospel and many more. Nothing is more enjoyable than listening to a talented musician or singer. Those with that talent are blessed and can do so much with that talent.

One of my small gifts came in the form of athletics and particularly baseball. I came from a baseball family and the game just seemed to come naturally to me. I had the pleasure of playing and coaching on various levels of the game. I made many friends as a result that I continue to see today. Although my talents are limited people skills can maximize the use of the gifts and talents that I do have.

Let's move on to the main point of this chapter. That is, people skills, or put another way the ability to communicate and function with other people positively. This is mostly accomplished through speech and sometimes body language.

The reason I bring this topic up is that if we are going to make a difference in this world, we must be able to communicate, negotiate, and participate with other people. I remember a professor of mine said that management is accomplishing things through and with other people. If we are going to work with other people to make good things happen then we must communicate with good and sound people skills.

Now what exactly would good people skills look like? The first thing would be the development of a positive rapport between the parties involved in the task or event. Maintaining good rapport creates a positive environment, increasing the likelihood of achieving the desired outcome successfully. I think the easiest way to do this is to always put yourself in the other person's shoes before speaking. How will they feel when you say or do what you are about to say or do?

Good people skills will carry a person a long way in life. How you react, what you say, and how you say it is very important when communicating with other people. As is the case with all skill sets, some people naturally have better people skills than others, but if a person can work to develop good people skills, life can be a little easier and less stressful. Who knows, one might learn, share, and benefit from those you meet along the way. This is not necessarily an easy task, but it is a very important aspect of coexisting in society.

I could write many pages on this topic but let me summarize with this. We are all different in many aspects of our make up. We have different thinking about things, a difference of opinion, different likes and dislikes, and lastly, we all come from different backgrounds and homelives. However, the one thing we have in common is that we are human beings created by God for a worldly purpose and for that reason we must respect each other as being that creation. Remember, none are better than others only different than others. This is difficult to adhere to, but if we work on our skills, we can become better at the task of managing those all-important people skills.

REMEMBER: IT IS YOUR LIFE WHAT IS NEXT?

Chapter Eight

LIFE STAGES

If we live long enough, we all go through stages of life. For the sake of this writing, I will define life in four stages and those are youth, young adulthood, middle age, and elderly. Each of these stages can be broken down into various times of life. As we dive into each stage, I will address each into substages for the sake of clarification relating to what is next in your life. As this is done you can decide on where you fall in the four stages and thus maybe start thinking about what could possibly be next for you.

Ok, let's look at our first stage which is youth. In my thinking, youth may range from birth to eighteen years of age. Naturally the younger a person is the less they are thinking about what is next in their life. If I had to guess, thinking seriously about the future may begin in the early teens. This will vary due to environment and maturity level as well as other factors. Lanning is different from person to person, but during the maturity process everyone starts to wonder about their future.

As a person starts to mature and experience life's ups, downs, and all around they start to think about where I am going, what is my purpose, and what do I do with my life, and maybe we can sum it up with the simple age-old question of what I want to be. Many times, we hear people ask a young person what do you want to be when you grow up. The answer may be something like a fireman or a policeman but often the answer is I don't know. There is usually no basis for this answer just a response of I don't know.

Some young adults are fortunate to know what they want to do early and start moving in that direction quickly and with purpose. How fortunate those people are. However, some and often many, people struggle with deciding about their future and flounder around for a while.

It is interesting to note that many high school seniors upon graduation are highly undecided and having difficulty in finding their career path. Again, with time and life experiences they usually find their way.

In answering the question of what is next, I mentioned that we all have purpose and God given talents and abilities. The key is putting them together for the sake of happiness and success.

This brings up a good question that was asked by my professor in a graduate class I was attending. If you are a young person reading this, you may consider the question and the answer to be noteworthy. The professor asked if money meant success. At that time in my life, I had a wife, two children, and living on a teacher's salary while also in graduate school and money, or the lack thereof, was a significant part of my life. His answer to the question rather startled me. He said that money does not necessarily mean success as real success is happiness and contentment. Although we need money and it is important, it may not be the most important factor. He made another statement, that at the time I struggled with, but now I understand. He said that your profession and your job should be an extension of play. Thus, just like a child going out to play in the morning we should be excited about going out to play as an adult each day and that is a large part of success. He also said that money will take care of itself, and I never forgot that. I truly believe that success is being happy, making a difference, and of course making a living.

Young people, don't worry about your future too early, but maybe you should just start thinking about what you like and are interested in. Pursue those areas and see where it takes you. At the proper time you will think more seriously about your career, the geographic location of where you want to live, and all the other grown-up decisions that come with life. I think that I mentioned earlier that I am a Christian and as a big part of my decision-making formula, I made God/Jesus my main advisor and it worked every time.

The next stage of this wonderful thing we call life is the young adult. For the sake of discussion let's put this in the age category from nineteen to forty-five. I know this is a large range, but due to the nature of the topic it will flow well.

The young adults are probably concerned more about their future than any other age category as they are building careers, starting families, and making decisions related to where they will live. They are starting to experience all of life. Therefore, the question about what is next is more concerning and they see that positive outcomes are obtained through forethought and planning. Thus, IT IS YOUR LIFE WHAT IS NEXT.

As a young adult experiences life, they can see the difficult things of life, the hardships of life, the surprises of life, and the beautiful things of life. It is like a young child learning that hot burns, sweet things usually taste good, and bad things are not good. So, navigating the many parts of life needs to be given thought, planning, and concern. With that said, one may determine the kind of person they are or want to be. Usually, people do not take time to assess this point, but it should be done. The kind of person you may relate to, how you treat others, what is your position on religion, what is your stance on social matters, how do you feel about politics, and there are many such topics and all of them could impact what is next in your life.

Well, concerning young adults this was a very short summary of that phase of life, but it is a very important part of our lifetime and making decisions related to IT IS MY LIFE WHAT IS NEXT with lasting outcomes.

The third stage of life that I am going to address is that of middle age. For the sake of this writing let's identify this range from age forty-six to sixty-five. This is another large span of age, but it will work as we discuss the topic, IT IS YOUR LIFE, WHAT IS NEXT, as there are many similarities in decision-making for this age group.

As we age, thoughts about the future change from that of our previously discussed age categories. More concern is given to things like enjoying (or not enjoying) the working environment, raising a family, affording the needs of that family, grandchildren, retirement, and other topics related to the not as young side of life. The thoughts of the future change as we age, and careful attention should be given to how a person can take the experiences of life and make them valuable to the future.

Often aging can cause a person to fall into a negative trap and become depressed, negative, and quite frankly not fun to be around. This usually occurs closer to the elderly and not so much with the younger side of middle age.

Middle age can be a great time of life as children are becoming more self-sufficient, fun to be with, and parents are hopefully seeing the fruits of their labor. Given all of the temptations in the world today this time of life may also be a difficult time as a parent. Hopefully, it will be short-lived with a good outcome.

Another area related to middle age and difficult times could be the parents of the middle-aged child are experiencing failing health which causes stress and heartache. Hopefully, this will not be the case and middle age is a great time to experience parents and children.

The middle age stage of life can be a wonderful time, a difficult time, or a combination of the two. Whatever the situation, it will absolutely be a time to ask the question, IT IS MY LIFE WHAT IS NEXT?

The fourth and final stage of life to be discussed is that of the elderly. Again, for the sake of this writing let's tag this age group as sixty-five and above. Many of us older folks avoid being called elderly, but we must accept that this is a stage of our life and it can be productive, exciting, and enjoyable. Elderly people have a great deal of knowledge and life experiences to share if only they take the time to do so.

I dare to say the greatest challenge for the elderly is health status. If a person is mobile and in general good health, great things can happen no matter what age category. If a person has some health issues maybe those can be worked around and that elderly person can make quite a contribution. It is amazing what can be done with our good healthcare system with respect to both the quality and longevity of life.

It is my opinion, that it is a real shame for a person of any age to become selfish, lazy, and unconcerned about making a difference. Remember, we were not put on this earth to breathe air, eat, and take up space. Everyone has talents and each of us should share those talents with others. An able-bodied elderly person should not sit in the rocking chair all day, complain about things, and have the attitude that I made mine now I am going to do nothing for the remainder of my life. Get up, get moving, and answer the great question, IT IS MY LIFE WHAT IS NEXT. As long as we have breath, something is next.

REMEMBER: IT IS YOUR LIFE WHAT IS NEXT?

Chapter Nine

THE IMPACT OF HEALTH

A very important part of life and how a person performs in their life is health. Generally, health is better at a young age and becomes progressively worse as we grow older. Younger people usually think less about their health, and probably about what is next in their life, than older people. As we age not only does our thinking change, but also our abilities from both a physical and a mental standpoint change. So how does this impact our decisions related to "IT'S YOUR LIFE WHAT IS NEXT"?

Well, the answer to the above question can be found somewhere in the chapter related to life's stages. As we age what is next, and what we desire to be next, will change and our health plays a major role in those decisions.

I know of many people that have life altering changes in their lives as a result of a change in their health. Some of them retired early, others changed professions, many became depressed and less functional, and some made the health issue a positive and began to respect life and each day more. Often health altering experiences change a person's attitude. Thus, they become more aware of the value of life and conclude that life's adventures and the people around them are more important than physical things valued in the past.

What is next in your life is very important. Also important is thoughtful planning about this question. Health status will play a major role in this planning process. If your health limits you physically then I doubt that cross-country running would be part of your planning for the next thing in your life. However, if one of your talents is teaching, then working with tutoring programs and the like could be a great opportunity for what is next. Afterall, it is your life, and you have control over it. We should not forget that we do have control and should use our intellectual and physical abilities to assess how we use this control to align our skills and interests to answer the question of what is next. Remember it is your life and you choose how to use it. You can use it for good things and the results could be happiness for you and others or you go the other way with an outcome of not so good.

Now back to health and the future. Many related things can impact and control our health. It is important to remember that good health decisions usually result in good health outcomes. We all know the negatives related to health like poor eating habits, overindulging in alcohol, too little exercise, and the like. I had a medical doctor tell me that he was not sure that healthy living resulted in a significant increase in longevity, but he was sure that healthy living resulted in a better quality of living over a lifetime. A better quality of living results in more opportunities to exercise our decisions related to what is next in our life.

Another factor of our health it is sad to say but, if we become unhealthy and have major issues, this does not just impact us. Bad health can impact our family, friends, co-workers and others that we encounter. So, something we should consider is how we manage and what attitudes do we have about our unhealthy situation. Many times, we can be an example of how to deal with such conditions which could impact those who observe our situation. Even in difficult times that we find ourselves in we are living what is next without even being aware of it.

The bottom line is let's take care of ourselves so that we can stay as healthy as possible and make a difference. The goal is to be healthy, but even when our health negatively changes, we can continue to make a difference, maybe just in another way that we had not planned on. The best laid plans often need to be altered and that is ok, we just make the adjustments and keep moving forward.

REMEMBER: IT IS YOUR LIFE WHAT IS NEXT?

Chapter Ten

WHAT ABOUT GOD, RELIGION, AND CHRISTIANITY

When we are looking into our book title "IT'S YOUR LIFE WHAT'S NEXT" it would be highly irresponsible of me not to dive into the greatest factor and influencer of all and that is God and religion. I may as well put my position, feelings, and beliefs out here right now as they are going to surface soon anyway. My position personally is that I am a Christian and a believer in Christian teachings. With that said, I would like to point out that I also believe that each person has the right and privilege of making their own decisions related to religious beliefs.

In fact, one of the strongest ideas written throughout the Bible is that a person has a choice concerning their relationship with God. Think about it, if we have no choice in a relationship with Him, then a forced relationship would be of no value. Therefore, if I am forced to be your friend, then I am probably not your friend, but if I chose to be your friend and you chose to be my friend then we have a true friendship. I believe that God wants a relationship with and loves each of us and there is nothing we can do about that other than decide about that relationship he offers us. Wow, that goes along with the title of this publication. Again, we decide and live with the consequences.

I had a little friend tell me that we need relationships, and that isolation is a bad thing. As I write this chapter, our country and the world are dealing with COVID 19. This virus has changed the way we live, socialize, work, and gather. It has caused a great deal of isolation with many sad outcomes. So yes, we need relationships. We are better together. Christian religions say that we are better with God than without him. Again, your decision.

Another matter that falls under the topic of this chapter is that we were created for a purpose, and we have value. We were not created and placed on this earth to take up space, breathe air, and eat food. Each of us has a talent and it is our responsibility to find that talent and put it to good use for mankind. Once our life is over hopefully, we can say that "I made a difference and a contribution to society, this world, and the ones I love". So, it is your life, and you can make decisions about what is next.

I would like to share a story about me and not my little friend this time. Just as I am sure you have experienced, I found myself early in life floundering around trying to find my purpose. It was a terrible time in my life and I was in total misery.

At the time, I had finished my bachelor's degree in education and thought I was going to be the greatest coach on the face of this earth. Coach Paul Bear Bryant move over and get ready because here comes the new coach in this world. Then reality hit me between the eyes and obtaining a job was not as easy as I thought it was going to be. I landed a job teaching in the high school I graduated from, but not coaching. I had to take this job as I was married, and we needed the money. So, I did, but I was miserable and that continued for about three years. I was offered a few jobs that seemed ok, but they didn't pan out. Then I was offered two coaching jobs, one in a high school and another in a middle school. As you probably can guess this highly motivated, well-versed, and hot-shot coach took the high school job. Well, it turned out to be one of the worst career decisions I ever made. The kids were great, the school was great, but me and the coaching staff didn't see things the same way so after one year, I resigned and took a job outside of education and moved my family to a larger city. This was a big thing for us. I felt in my heart that this was not a good decision, and I went against my Godly feelings.

After relocating and working at the new position for a month, I was waiting and looking forward to my first big time paycheck outside of the education field and it arrived. That was great, BUT it did not clear the bank and the fast-talking guy that hired me had authorized a hot and NSF check. My goodness a family to care for and I am holding a bad payroll check.

I removed myself from that bad position and found me and my family in a new city with no job, no income, and limited savings. I kept feeling the tug that was bringing me back to the field of education and I was struggling with it. I wanted the opportunity for big money and a big position. That big ego and selfishness was getting the best of me.

So, what did I do? I will tell you exactly what I did. Remember, I said that life is better with God than without him. Well, I put my silly pride away, found a quiet place, and had a visit with the all-powerful Lord. I admitted my shortcomings, one of which was not listening, begged for forgiveness, and asked for direction.

To some people that may seem strange, but I can tell you at that point I felt a load removed from my shoulders and things started to turn around. The story is long and wonderful, but let me summarize. I found a job working in education, which is a story within itself as I started an adult education program for Native Americans in the state of Louisiana and we made a positive difference in many lives. Through this adventure I met an educator (one of my little friends) who made a significant impact in my life. As mentioned earlier, a weight was lifted from my shoulders and I was happy, content and making a difference. It just doesn't get any better than that.

Following this adventure, I was given many opportunities in the field of education to contribute. I will not go into detail with each, but I would like to list a few for the purpose of showing how important and valuable that day was when I called on my Lord Jesus to help me decide what is next in my life. Those examples are as follows.

1. Teaching and coaching at various schools (public and private)
2. Teaching in a prison setting (I was not an inmate ha.)
3. Teaching in a technical and vocational school
4. Teacher/administrator for a high-risk student program
5. School administration and supervision
6. Adjunct professor for a private college

So, as you can see, I have been blessed with opportunities to make a difference. Thank God for that NSF payroll check that seemed to be a disaster but turned into a blessing. I remember hearing a statement that gave me such insight into my shortcomings. It went something like, "The messes we make often turn out to be messages if we allow them to do so".

I am not finished with what was next for me. After all it is my life, and I must make decisions about the future and live with the consequences.

Just as I felt the tug to return to the field of education, I started to feel that same tug and influence that my time was coming to an end for me in the field of education. Oh, my goodness now what?

Well, it happened and here I am back before God asking what now? I have this little friend who told me to never forget that God works in mysterious ways, and He is always in control. As I look back over my lifetime, I find that to be so true.

I felt the tug, have been down this road before, and without a job again I decided to retire, after twenty-five years of service, in the school system. This was truly what you can call a leap of faith. The reason I say that is I had two kids in college, normal living expenses, and a very small monthly retirement check. My wife, Glynna, was working at the public library which helped. I didn't know what was next, but I knew he had something in mind.

My secretary in the school system asked me what I was going to do, and I told her I had no clue. She said that her son was the state marketing manager for a large health insurance company, and they were looking for a salesperson. I said no thank you as insurance selling to me seemed like high pressure sales and that is not me. She asked if he could take me to lunch and explain the details related to the position. To make a long story short, after two lunches and a couple of hands-on experiences with him, I said OK I will give it a try. After all I had nothing else going for me.

I took $25,000 from my retirement plan, put it in savings and promised myself I would use this money to maintain my family's existing standard of living and when it was depleted, I would get out of sales and get a real job.

To my astonishment, I found the selling of health insurance both rewarding and satisfying. It was more like a consulting job in which you helped individuals, families, and businesses with a very important need for all concerned. I became good at it and extremely happy in my new profession. In fact, I continue to help people in this area to this very day after twenty-five years in the industry.

Just a little bit more about my career in this area and how God works in mysterious ways. After my son obtained his degree, he began the process we all go through of trying to find ourselves. He came to me numerous times wanting to go into business with me, but I turned him away. I wanted him to experience the ups, downs, all-around, and pains of the real world. I did not give him the soft path to success as this would not be good for either of us.

One day, he came to me and said Dad, "If you won't let me work with you, then I am going to try it on my own". His wife is a nurse, and they had no children at the time, so this was perfect timing for him to take a risk.

We worked out an agreement of no salary, you eat what you kill, and we will see what happens. Well, it turned out to be one of the best business decisions either of us ever made. After working together for many years, we can say that all is well, and we never had an argument. This is because we set some ground rules at the beginning that we both could live with.

This is just another example of how He works in mysterious ways and if we listen and pay attention, He will never give us a bad direction even though sometimes we will question.

Well, after giving you the details I have experienced, I have one more to throw out there. I am feeling the tug once again and I have no idea where it will lead, but I am very excited about the possibilities. Stay tuned and we will see what happens.

I would like to finalize this chapter with a few statements related to life and finding one's way as it relates to God. Life can be difficult. It is like bamboo woven handcuffs, the more you pull and resist, the tighter they become. The trick is to loosen up and they will slide off easily. When we totally let go and let Him take control things get much better.

I would like to share another short list with you that hopefully will help you with knowing about your life and deciding what is next. They are as follows.

1. Give Him a chance to have a relationship with you.
2. Be careful about everything being about you.
3. He is the only one that can meet your needs.

4. Selfishness never satisfies but rather destroys.
5. Take some time and read the book of Proverbs.
6. Spend time and read scripture patiently.

I would like to conclude this chapter by saying that we all make mistakes, we all sin and do wrong, but for each mistake and wrong that we make He still loves us and is there to help along the way of what is next.

REMEMBER: IT IS YOUR LIFE WHAT IS NEXT?

Chapter Eleven

FORGIVENESS

This chapter will be short and to the point, although the topic is important it is best addressed straightforwardly. I don't feel that forgiveness is an emotion or a feeling, rather it is an experience and process that was brought about probably through emotions and when addressed will result in further emotions that will hopefully be positive ones.

Forgiveness is a word that is difficult for us to deal with followed by an action that sometimes feels impossible and uncomfortable. Often, we must admit wrongdoing, accept things for what they are, let the past be the past, soften our hearts, and be willing to accept or give an apology. Forgiveness is very important in considering our question of WHAT IS NEXT in our life and moving on with peace and purpose.

Grudges, hate, etc. are things that impair judgement, do not allow us to be compassionate for others, distort sound thinking, and just gets in the way of relationships. Forgiveness corrects these things and puts decision-making and relationships back on a sound and positive track.

The act of forgiving is a wonderful and fulfilling experience. People often say that it takes a load off them with positive outcomes for the short- and long-term future. The Bible is all about forgiveness and its value. Jesus is the ultimate act of forgiveness. Maybe we should make more of an effort to be like Him. Although impossible, when we get closer our lives and relationships improve.

When we consider forgiveness and the WHAT IS NEXT decision, many doors can be opened as a result of forgiving someone. Contrary to some thinking, quite often both parties have deep down desires to experience forgiveness. All involved know that working together in harmony is much better than the agony of conflict. The problem causing the conflict is like a dark cloud hanging over us and as with any other cloud the results are usually thunder and lightning.

I mentioned doors that can be opened because of forgiveness and this can include renewed friendships, professional agreement, families coming together, and just an overall better environment for all resulting in a peaceful coexistence and a better life. When that peacefulness is experienced the question of WHAT IS NEXT may take on a completely different meaning from that which could have been without that forgiveness.

Putting our main question aside, forgiveness is a beautiful thing with usually good outcomes. I think the key to forgiveness is not to wait too long because the old saying about "time heals all wounds" is not always true. Although timing has its place in forgiving, we should not take too much of it as there is also another term called festering which can be very detrimental to the forgiveness process. I truly believe that the matters related to the issues should be addressed sooner rather than later. I have found that solving issues between humans is usually done best with honesty, love, concern, and a desire to solve conflicts. When this approach is taken, often the issue or issues are resolved with positive outcomes.

I would like to complete this topic with a word of advice which is don't be afraid to forgive or be forgiven. Forgiveness is a beautiful thing with long-term benefits. Who knows, your future may depend on it.

REMEMBER: IT'S YOUR LIFE WHAT IS NEXT?

Chapter Twelve

WHAT ABOUT TECHNOLOGY

The subject of technology is something that came on the scene not too long ago and continues to expand its capabilities by the minute. With respect to decision making and topic research, technology is invaluable. In the old days we used something called encyclopedias which was a volume of books listed A to Z and were out of date at the time of printing, but that is all we had for historical data. As a kid in school when you were assigned a report, the encyclopedias were the source of information.

Concerning our question "ITS YOUR LIFE WHAT IS NEXT?" technology is a great source of information. As we all know technology has good points and bad. In researching our question, we must be very cautious in obtaining sound, valuable, and correct information. Good decisions are the result of good information.

I am highly concerned about how our society has become so technology-dependent. My family members, friends, and business associates are all technology super connected. The smartphone is addictive. In the old days, and I am not saying the old days were perfect by any means, a businessman went to lunch without a smartphone. He did not receive any messages until he returned to the office, and they were written on either a notepad or the fancy message forms that came in duplicate. Families shared meals and had discussions without any interruptions. No one got up and left the group to take that all important call. The phone has become number one and all else takes a back seat. Is that good and are all those calls, texts, or emails important enough to take precedence over the task at hand or the people you are talking to? Maybe or maybe not. Is technology causing a great deal of stress in our lives?

Just one more thing to date myself and share a little bit of history. When I was a kid, we had something called a party line with our phones. Oh, by the way, we had only one phone in the house, and it probably weighed over ten pounds. The party line was a system of rings, maybe one, two, or three, which indicated if the call was for you or the other neighbors sharing the line. Yes, you could listen to other people's calls. What a fun thing to do as a youngster until you got caught. Privacy has taken on a completely different meaning today as compared to the past.

Let's talk about how technology can be valuable in answering our questions. First, it provides almost endless information. Whether we are searching for careers, health conditions, or looking for a good restaurant the information is readily available. It is easy to find information quickly.

However, remember that it is important to obtain information that is sound and factual.

I certainly encourage everyone to use all sources available to assist in answering the question which includes technology, but this source alone is not the final answer. This brings me to the matter of what are all-inclusive sources that I should use to find the answer to our big question “IT IS YOUR LIFE WHAT IS NEXT”. I would like to list and discuss the ones that I think are important. I guess we could call them the formula, or outline, to answer our big question.

Let’s do a crazy thing that may help in remembering the sources. We can list the first letter of each source to be considered in the answer. How about GOTGEL (better known as an acronym)? Wow what a word or maybe not a word. I hope it helps. Each letter will give us a source to refer to when making our decision.

Our new word GOTGEL is something that we need to break down and discuss. The letters are not in any order other than the first one. So, let’s get started.

The first letter “G” stands for, you guessed it, God. The reason I chose this letter first is that my beliefs tell me that God is the creator, all knowing, and the greatest counselor anyone could ask for. All other sources are secondary, but topics that need to be addressed. Each time in my life that I took total control, things got messy. However, we should remember that every mess results in a message if we allow it to do so. As we consider all parts of our new word, let's not forget about the Great Counselor.

The second letter is "O" which stands for outcomes. After all our ultimate objective in this questioning process is the outcome. We desire to have a positive outcome with positive consequences. When we have completed the process found in our new word GOTGEL our answer hopefully will be our decision relative to what is next in our life or at least a good direction followed by actions we experience.

The third letter is "T" which stands for technology. As mentioned earlier, technology is valuable and when used properly can assist us greatly in answering our questions related to what is next in our life.

The fourth letter is another "G" which stands for our gut feelings. Contrary to some schools of thought our gut feelings carry a tremendous amount of weight in decision making. That inside feeling that is difficult to explain, but you are certain is present, should never be overlooked in the process.

The fifth letter is "E" which represents our experiences. Experiential learning is one of the most important ways that we learn. A simple example would be telling little Johnny not to touch that fire as it is hot. Little Johnny ignores the warning and touches the hot fire and instantly finds out what experiential learning is all about. Our experiences teach us many things, and this continues as we go through life. Thus, use your life experiences when deciding what is next.

Our final letter of our new word is “L” which gives us our likes and dislikes. If you like something, you will probably be successful at it and just the opposite if you dislike something. In making your decision about what is next, consideration must be given to both your likes and dislikes.

The reason I included GOTGEL in this chapter is that I wanted to make sure that all understand the position that technology plays in decision-making and make the point that our decision about what is next includes a great deal more than a computer and the data it provides. Use all your tools in the process and remember to always weigh the balance between cost versus benefit. Be careful that the costs don’t outweigh the benefits as you always want good things to be in your future.

REMEMBER: IT IS YOUR LIFE WHAT IS NEXT?

Chapter Thirteen

THE IMPACT OF GOVERNMENT

This chapter is going to address a topic that each of us has limited control over and that is government. Government, whether we like it or not, does exist and has both a positive and negative impact on our lives. This impact does affect what is next from both the short and long-run prospective. When considering and planning for what is next in one's life consideration should be given to government influences and how that can affect decision making and planning.

Let's make a short list of related topics as follows:

1. Regulations
2. Funding Opportunities
3. Available Information
4. Taxes

Now we need to address each one in a little more detail. Please note that this is not an exhaustive list and I encourage you to spend more time in this area as you move closer to specifics related to your plans concerning what is next in your life.

Regulations make up a very large part in the role that government plays in our world today. These regulations may apply to federal, state, and local governments. Over time regulations have become greater in number and more specific in control of daily life as we know it today. Government regulations control many things from transportation to tax rates and will probably have some impact on all our future decisions. This impact could fall into that of taxation, regulating your product or service, environmental issues, employees, and many others. We should do our research to see how these regulations impact decision making.

We need to remember and consider that not all regulations are bad. Many have good objectives with positive outcomes. Can you imagine having our country operating daily without federal, state, and local laws relative to human behavior such as domestic violence, robbery, murder and the like. However, some regulations feel to be a nuisance and just crazy. If we find ourselves in this position, we have two options. Those options are to work on getting them rectified through proper channels or live with it and move on. That idea of living with it and moving on seems a little strange and almost un-American, but sometimes it can be a viable option.

Another impact the government has which is a good one if you fall into the receiving side of it and that is funding opportunities. Should you have a business opportunity or project that could qualify, then government funding may be available to assist you. Funding could come in the form of a loan, grant, or scholarship. This is a very important area that we all may consider in some phase of our decision-making process as government funding could assist from school loans to small business lending. I suggest you do your homework on this one. There is a tremendous number of publications, websites, etc. to assist in your research.

Another influence is that of information. Not only can the government provide information related to your planning process, but it can also provide you with ideas that may energize you toward selecting that topic. Let's face it, today's world has more information available than ever and if we are smart, we can put that information to work for us. Good, sound, legal, and ethical information can result in smart decisions with great consequences. Work smart, obtain good info, and do good things. Wow, if more people did that, we could make the world a better place. What a wonderful thought.

Well, I stated earlier that not all regulations are bad, and I continue to stand by that thought. However, I would now like to discuss the fourth topic of regulations and that is taxes. I think all of us cringe when it comes to tax time. We feel we are paying too much and there is a constant battle between government leadership and the taxpayers as to how much is fair. Most people realize that the government must have money to operate, but the rub comes with the question of how the money is spent, which has always been and will continue to be a controversial subject.

As part of your decisions about the future, taxation will be a factor. If that is the case, I suggest you find a good and ethical tax professional to assist you. So often, a person can make a great decision about the future, move forward and be productive, and then find themselves in a crisis with respect to taxation. Don't let that happen to you, do it correctly from the start.

With respect to the government's impact on the topic, IT'S YOUR LIFE WHAT IS NEXT, I suggest you learn as much as you can about it and find out what impact you may experience, take advantage of how the government can assist in reaching your goals, and play by the rules. Who knows, the outcome could be great for you and many others.

REMEMBER: IT'S YOUR LIFE WHAT IS NEXT?

Chapter Fourteen

THE VALUE OF A MENTOR

In the world we live in today, a vast amount of information and choices are available to all who seek them. This can cause the decision-making process to become very difficult and complicated. We have a tremendous amount of data at our disposal quickly. If you recall earlier in my writing, I referred to the encyclopedia as a source of information back in the day. This method was extremely time-consuming and became outdated quickly. Today this is not the case.

Due to the number of published topics and other means of sharing information via cell phone conversations, texting, and other technology we can find ourselves with a tremendous amount of data that may assist us in the decision-making process or put us in a confusing position. Because of this and other factors that may relate to researching topics, including *what is next in our life*, we could probably use another source called a mentor. This wonderful person may come in the form of a friend, parent, spouse, sibling, fellow worker, minister, teacher, coach, religious teacher or any other person that you know, trust, and respect their opinions.

I have had many mentors throughout my life and each of them played a major role in the direction my life has taken. Some helped me professionally, some helped me raise my family, some helped me spiritually, and some helped me when times were both good and bad. I cannot stress enough as to the value of those people to me. It is often difficult to share your thoughts and feelings with another person. That is why it is important to select a mentor that you feel extremely comfortable with and trust completely. Often it takes a while to develop the mentor relationship and you will know when that relationship has reached the point of mentorship.

A solid mentor can help you make critical decisions, way the pros and cons of a situation, assist in doing the correct thing, decide on a moral dilemma, and many other aspects of your life that need a solid and good outcome. We should value that mentor relationship and never compromise it. I feel that mentors fall into the category of angels from heaven. They can carry such a powerful bit of knowledge and insight. If we are wise, we should take this mentorship opportunity and put it to work in our lives.

Here is a thought, maybe we will have the opportunity to not only receive the value of a mentor, but also to become a mentor to someone. Young people can befriend and mentor other young people. Middle-aged and older people can mentor others as they have much knowledge from life experiences that they can share. Just a note to remember that should you become a mentor to someone, you are taking on an awesome responsibility and this task should not be taken lightly. That relationship should be one of honesty, integrity, and with the purpose of having a positive influence on the one being mentored.

Often becoming a mentor helps both parties with identifying, understanding, and solving problems or confronting an issue. As the old saying goes, sometimes you learn more as a teacher than you did as a student. How well I know this.

There are barriers to overcome on both sides of the mentoring relationship. Some of these can be age differences, a difference in thinking about life, or at first impressions not agreeing on certain things. These barriers can be managed if a common goal of working together for the betterment of someone or something is agreed upon.

To summarize the value of a mentor I would just like to say don't be afraid to reach out on both sides of the mentoring relationship. There is value in obtaining knowledge and wisdom from a good mentor. Also, there is value in being a good mentor. Either way mentorship has its place in the development of a person, and we should take advantage of this asset as often as possible.

REMEMBER: IT IS YOUR LIFE WHAT IS NEXT?

Chapter Fifteen

FAILURES AND DISAPPOINTMENTS

The first thing I want to address is accomplishments and the reason for doing so is not to boast, be arrogant, etc., but rather to make a point that although I have had my challenges, good things can be achieved as we go through life. We all can make a difference. I also want to note that not everything in my life, and I suspect yours also has been rosy, easy, and with great outcomes. Even the Bible says that our lives will not always be easy. By addressing accomplishments along with difficulties and failures, the point is to ask the question, what is next?

We should plan and work the plan knowing that we will experience both negative and positive outcomes because of living life. Remember, something is always next and all of us have input and control over the answer to that question. You know the question.

I feel that the most appropriate format for easy reading, with respect to my accomplishments, is to present a few of them with respect to how they have been influential in my life. I will spend a little time on each for clarity. The purpose of my examples is to make the point that life can be good.

The first one is what I would call my miracle birth. I was born in 1949 and my parents were older (Dad 40 and Mother 37). Of course, I can only present my situation as others have told me. In 1949 a thirty-seven-year-old woman having a baby was risky. I understand that my mother was told initially that she had a tumor and then after further examination and time it was determined that she was indeed pregnant. During that period medical testing and evaluation were limited. Therefore, the one hundred percent assessment of the baby's sex, or the health could only be realized at birth. I understand that I was born prematurely, very small, and with an undeveloped twin. As the story goes much concern and anxiety was experienced by all. With all of that said, I was blessed to grow into a healthy child and adult. Thank God for that.

Therefore, my first accomplishment, totally under the control of God through the assistance of others, was birth. Birth is a miracle and accomplishment within itself, but mine came with a little twist.

The second accomplishment that I would like to present is family. As mentioned previously, I have been absolutely blessed with a great family. Notice I did not say perfect, I said great. All families have issues over time, but great families work on those issues with a common goal of solving them. We have worked and solved most of them but as always with any relationship there is a little more work to be done.

When I talk about family, I mean parents (Munnie Gal and Daddy Boy). We were so blessed to have good, strong, God-fearing, Christian parents. I could write another complete book on this topic, but for now we will just say they were great parents and that was a good start for me and my siblings.

On the topic of siblings, I have two sisters (Sue and Lena Ann). They were both much older than me and seemed to be more like a parent than a sister. As they both grew up, moved along, and became good parents themselves, I was left at home, and I almost felt like an only child. The great thing was that my sister's offspring became almost like my brother and sisters as we were close in age. Growing up was good and I could share many stories, tales, and yarns about it, but I will spare readers from that.

The second phase of my family is my immediate family. As I mentioned in another part of this writing about meeting, falling in love with, and marrying my wife, Glynna. We have been married for over fifty years and we know it is going to work out. What a great fifty years and we are hoping for many more. As the result of our love and marriage, we have been blessed with two children (Kim and Will) along with five grandchildren (Taylor, Ella, Brooks, Carter, and Cullynn) and two wonderful in-laws (Kristen and Bill) who both have been good to and good for my children and grandchildren. Again, I could talk about many adventures with all, but I will keep them to myself and enjoy them personally.

The third accomplishment that I would like to share is that of my professional life. After completing my degree, I started teaching and I had the great opportunity to teach numerous subjects at different levels from elementary to secondary and beyond. These years were some of my favorites although they came with challenges along with rewards. After twenty-five years, it came time for me to retire and ask the question IT IS MY LIFE WHAT IS NEXT? That next was moving into business for myself. Later my son joined me and that has been over twenty-five years of my life and it too has been another great adventure and I continue that adventure to the day of this writing. However, I am starting to ask myself the question IT IS MY LIFE AND WHAT IS NEXT and just maybe it could be related to writing and speaking, who knows?

The fourth accomplishment is not necessarily an accomplishment, but rather a super blessing. That is how the Lord Jesus has influenced and guided my life. I can't tell you how many times I have run off the rails, made bad decisions, and just lived my life poorly and went down the wrong path. Each time "I" took complete control and did things my way without fail, a mess would occur. Each time I went the wrong way and got into trouble, I never forgot that God said that He would never leave or forsake me and that is so true. Each time I sought His counsel and His direction, I was forgiven and put back on the true path. With that said maybe the question should be that it is my life (under His guidance) and what does He want me to do next. Now that is something to be thought about.

After discussing my few handpicked successes, I would like to present a few of the things that were not easy and were challenging. These would be some of my failures and disappointments. Each of us will experience these things and I think the most important takeaway is not what happens, but rather how we handle what happens. We should remember that others are watching, and a good positive influence carries a ton of weight.

The first thing, and one that we all must deal with at some point in our life, is death. I have experienced both sudden and unexpected deaths of family members and friends. None of them were easy or without sadness and pain.

The sudden ones came as car accidents, heart attacks, suicides, and the like. Others were related to Alzheimer's, dimensions, cancer, and other long-range illnesses. Of course, the most personal and difficult ones are the people that were closest to you and this pain carries on for years if not a lifetime. These experiences can have a strong impact on the surviving person's ability to think, function, and plan. These results can be both long-term and short-term. Concerning the question of whether it is your life what is next, the impact of death can be quite influential from both a negative and positive position. Although difficult to say, and even more to live, this is a time that we must continue with life and make life's decisions.

The second topic concerning the difficulties of life could be either experiencing or the fear of failure. Failure is something all of us try to avoid. The reason for that is we don't want to be embarrassed, lose money, let someone down, or many other reasons that cause us to try and avoid failure.

Failure can also affect how we approach our question; it is your life and what's next. If we have failed at something, we may go in another direction in the future and not want to climb back on that horse again and try to ride it. If that is our attitude, we may be missing out on something good as often time failures make us stronger. Most successful people have failed many times. The only problem with this is that people tend to only remember the successes. An example of this goes way back in time, but there was a magical and mystical baseball player who played for the New York Yankees by the name of Babe Ruth. For many years he held the record for the most home runs in a single season with that number being sixty. However, many people don't know that he also held the record for the most strikeouts. With that large number of strikeouts had Babe quit baseball that would have been a shame for him, others, and baseball. Sometimes failures are good.

The third and final example of how life can be challenging is that of disappointment. We make our plans, set our standards, and work hard toward a goal and it does not work out. This outcome is really heartbreaking and difficult to deal with. This is one of those times in life that makes us stronger although it doesn't feel that way at the time.

Like many young kids, I had a dream of becoming a major league baseball player, maybe like Babe Ruth who knows. I could just see myself in the bright lights with fame and fortune. At the time, I had no realistic idea of what it took to get there, stay there, and earn all the perks. I just knew that was what I wanted to do. In my support, I worked hard at it, dreamed about it, and did all I could at the time to prepare myself. My total focus was on that prize.

As I grew, matured, and experienced life with and outside of baseball I became aware of the obstacles, challenges, and realities related to my goal. Later in life during my coaching days when I was wiser and more aware of things, I shared with my players, no matter what the sport, that you should play the game if you have the ability and the want to. I also told them that those two variables are different for each person. Many have a long career and others a shorter career. Often time injuries come into play. This is really where our question is important relative to it's your life what is next comes into play?

My original goal did not work out and that was very disappointing. Still, once I overcame the heartbreak, I realized that this is a big old world and many exciting opportunities are available. I just needed to find them, and I did. I am now happy and content and look forward to my future experiences.

Therefore, as can be seen in my little examples of the ups, downs, and all arounds of life, we all need to spend time asking the question “IT’S MY LIFE WHAT IS NEXT”.

I would also like to note that each life is different in that some have a good family, others don’t, many find a grand opportunity that seems to fall in their laps, and others don’t, many just seem to have it made, and others don’t, but no matter what the circumstances are we can know a few things for certain. Arrogance is bad, hard work is good, we have much control over our future, self-pity gets in the way, and God loves us, and we need to lean on him for guidance.

REMEMBER: IT’S YOUR LIFE WHAT’S NEXT?

Chapter Sixteen

DEATH

I guess it is appropriate to make the final chapter about death as this is the last function we will have on this earth as human beings. As defined by WEBSTER'S, death is the cessation of all vital functions and the end of life. From this definition we can assume that the body ceases to function in any form or fashion and life on this earth for our body no longer exists. Therefore, the old saying that we can't get out of this world alive certainly applies to all of us.

The main topic of our discussion is IT'S YOUR LIFE WHAT IS NEXT, takes on a whole new meaning when the new topic of death is considered. What is next on this earth is nothing, null, void, and nonexistent. Therefore, what is next per the ideas, beliefs, and opinions of human beings, both past and present, may vary. We Christians believe that the future is brighter than ever, and a paradise is ahead of us and will be wonderful forever. Others may believe that when it is over, it is over and yet some are confused with no thoughts or ideas at all about life after death. They just leave that to chance.

This topic has been one of discussion since the beginning of time. Much speculation has been made about the hereafter and what happens at death. Some say they have even experienced death, saw a white light, a tunnel, and felt a wonderful feeling of euphoria. Nothing has been proven about these experiences and the mystery continues.

In 2 Corinthians 5:6-8 it is written that, “so we are always confident, because we know that while we are living in the body, we are away from our home with the Lord. We live by faith and not by sight. We are confident, and we would prefer to leave the body and to be at home with the Lord.” This passage of scripture does not mean we are to take our own life or anyone else’s, but I feel that it means we should be happy and know that he has prepared a place for us, and we should not fear death.

When we experience death on this earth, then hopefully as mentioned in Chapter Fourteen that our life had a purpose and we contributed to making our environment a little better for the people in it. If you think about it maybe our decisions along the way about WHAT IS NEXT may culminate at death and just maybe, also mentioned earlier, that our life was much more than breathing, eating, and taking up space. Hopefully, our life had great value. This is an important matter to consider as we are searching for a direction and manipulating our way through life. Remember, it will come to an end and at that point we can no longer make any changes related to who we were or what we did.

Thus, demonstrates the importance of decision-making relative to WHAT IS NEXT. This topic should never be taken lightly or without passion. It is important to you as good planning and decisions will result in a good and productive life. It is also important to others, as you may make a difference in their situation resulting in a better and more productive life for them.

None of us like to think about death and in the back of our mind somewhere we feel that we will live forever, and the subject does not apply to us. This is especially true when we are young. As we get older and experience the death of loved ones, friends, co-workers, and associates, the reality seems to become clearer and closer to us.

I remember when my mother's health was failing and death was close, she and I discussed the topic. We both agreed that if we truly believe what we say we believe that she was approaching the good part and I was going to be left with the worries, concerns, and troubles of the world. Don't misunderstand what we were saying, in that none of us want to end our lives too soon as we have things to do, a family to love and see grow, as well as experiencing life itself. Remember the ups, downs and all arounds of life can be so rewarding and at the same time challenging. Again, this is where WHAT IS NEXT becomes so important. We need to strive to make good decisions with good outcomes as we give emphasis to our central theme of IT'S YOUR LIFE WHAT IS NEXT.

I am going to finalize this chapter by saying that death is imminent, and we should be prepared for it but also life is imminent, and we should also be prepared for it. Both life and death follow the roadmap that God has prepared for humanity in that we will live and die. I will summarize by saying that we should be aware of and make decisions relative to both. As we go through life, we should think about, plan, and prepare for it with the overall objective of making life good, valuable, productive, and as happy as it can be. While also we need to remember that death is imminent, and we should prepare for it. As I see it, reading about and developing a relationship with the Trinity is so important and many people are either not interested or just don't care. Before you turn away from this activity, give it a try as you may be surprised at what you could learn and experience about death and the hereafter. This is the only homework I will give and that is if you don't know what the Trinity is look it up.

This chapter was probably not one that when looking at the table of contents, you would hurry and jump to and read, but it is important and must be discussed as it is a very big part of IT'S YOUR LIFE WHAT IS NEXT. Hopefully it did prompt you to think about a long-range future that we all must experience.

REMEMBER: IT'S YOUR LIFE WHAT IS NEXT?

CONCLUSION

Well, here we are after much thought and time related to the great question, "IT IS YOUR LIFE WHAT IS NEXT". Thanks for reading my project and I hope it will be food for thought for you and anyone you would like to share it with. We have brought to light many related topics from what life is to what has been accomplished in our lives. I think we have covered quite a bit of territory while considering the future and what it may hold. If we really put our minds to it, the future could be exciting with a tremendous number of opportunities to do something good and wonderful. That would be a great thing.

As we consider these good things and possibilities, I would like to take the liberty of listing a few of them that any of us could select from. Now remember, this is not an exhausting or perfect list but rather some things to think about. The list goes as follows:

1. Charity work
2. Volunteering
3. Changing professional direction
4. Learning something new to share
5. Read and research more
6. Start a religious study

7. Obtain a hobby

8. Find out things that make you really happy

9. Ask the question, how I can help people

10. Really think about what is next in your life

In the dedication section of my writing, I mentioned many who have influenced me, but you may find it strange that I have one more to say thanks to and that is my beloved German Shepard named Lady. She has been by my side throughout this wonderful adventure. Her part is to lie on the floor and keep me calm as I search for the proper words related to the topic at hand. She has done a great job with that and as I write this, she is calmly stretched out waiting for the call. What a great girl.

I have spent all this time and energy asking everyone to consider our question of what is next and now it is time for me to practice what I preach. I have been giving the question a great deal of thought and I will give you a sneak peek at my decision. I would like to find a format that would allow me to ask our question to many people. Hopefully that will include speaking to a wide variety of age groups from young to old.

In addition to that I would also like to partner with an old friend in developing coaches within the area of youth sports. Wow what a great challenge and opportunity. I bet you didn't see that one coming and I hope we can make it happen. So, stay tuned and we can see how exciting the future can be.

From Lady and I, we ask the great question to you:

"IT'S YOUR LIFE WHAT IS NEXT?"